I0390599

The Vintage Car & Truck Adult Coloring Book

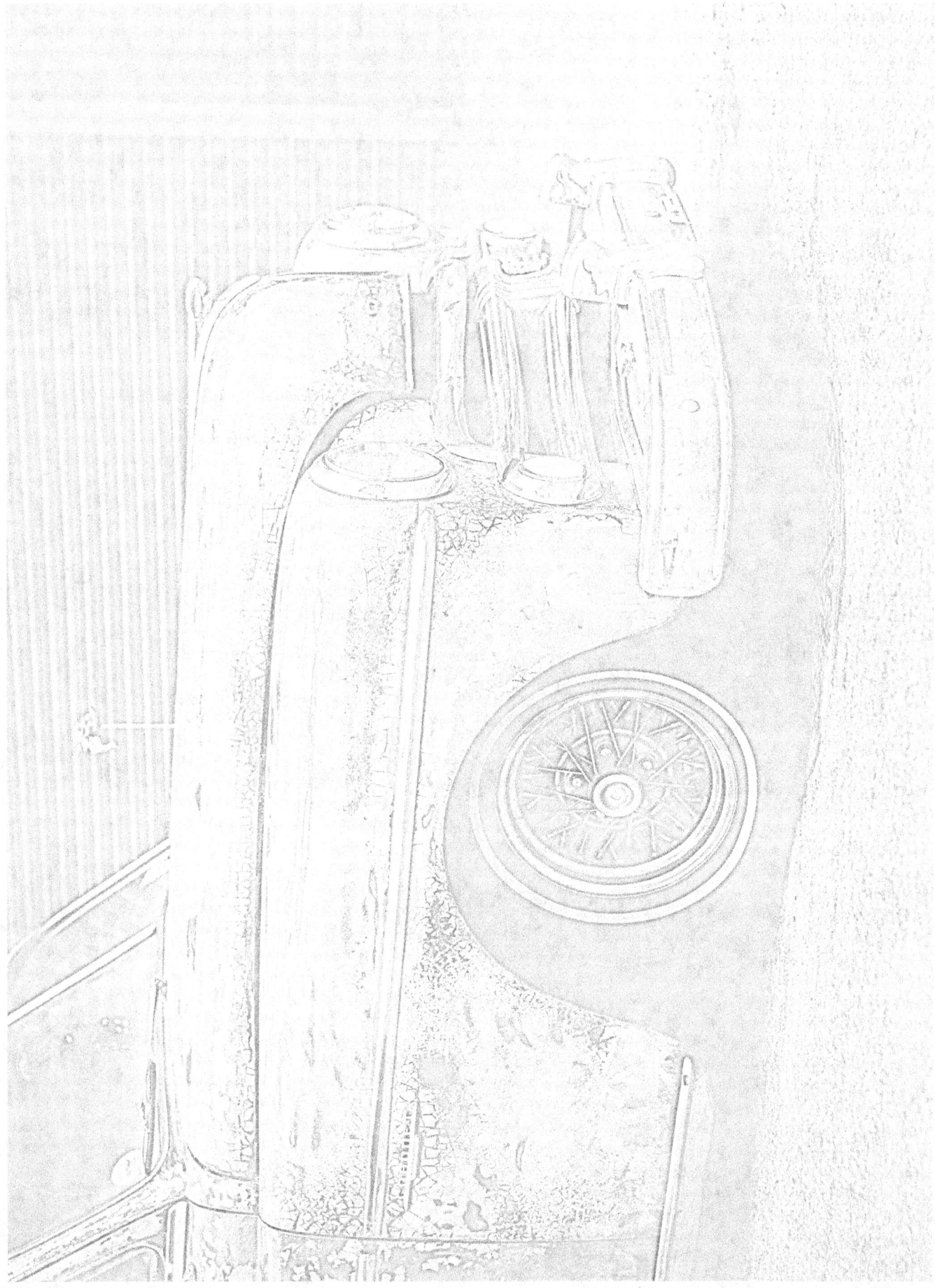

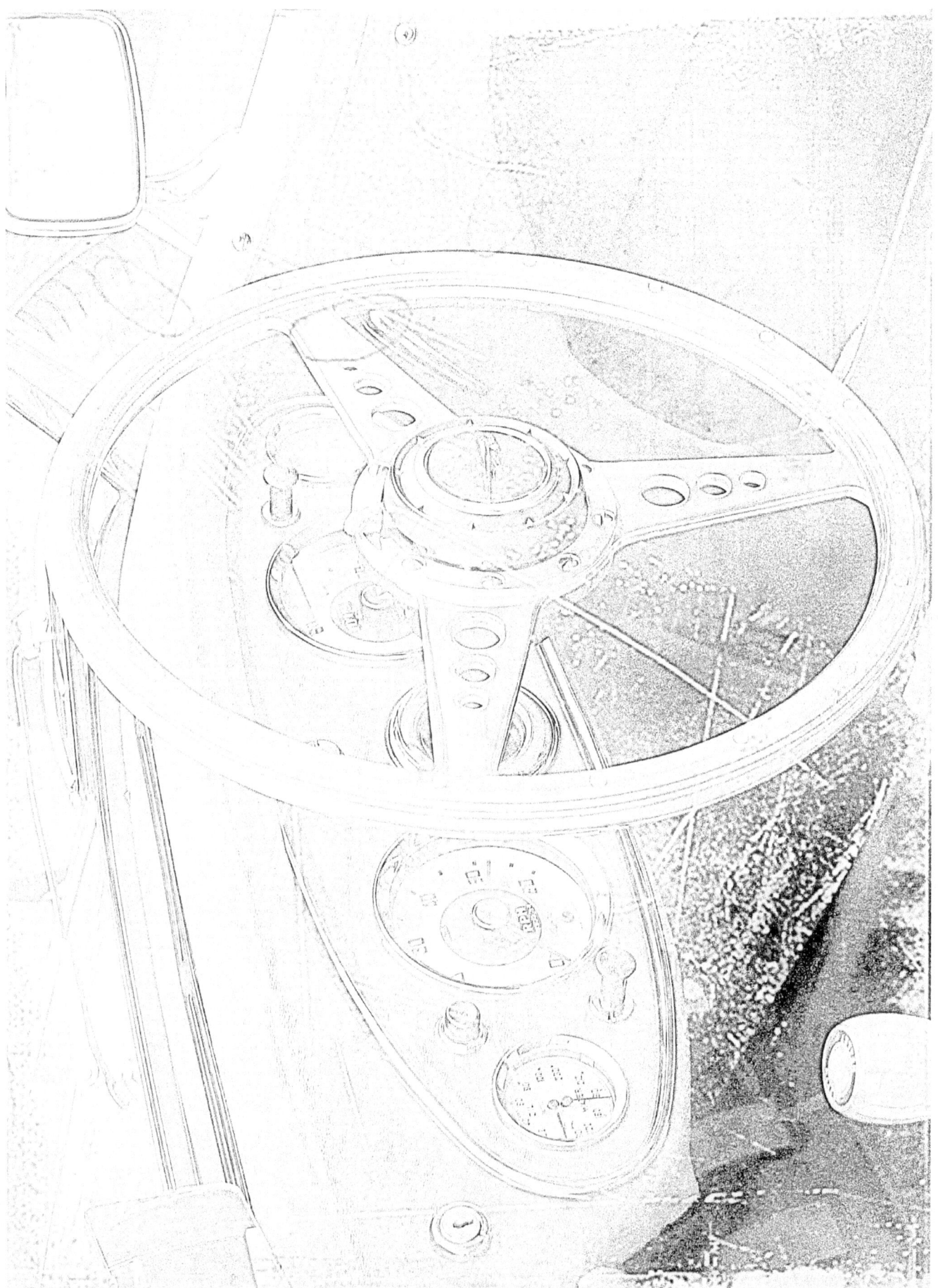

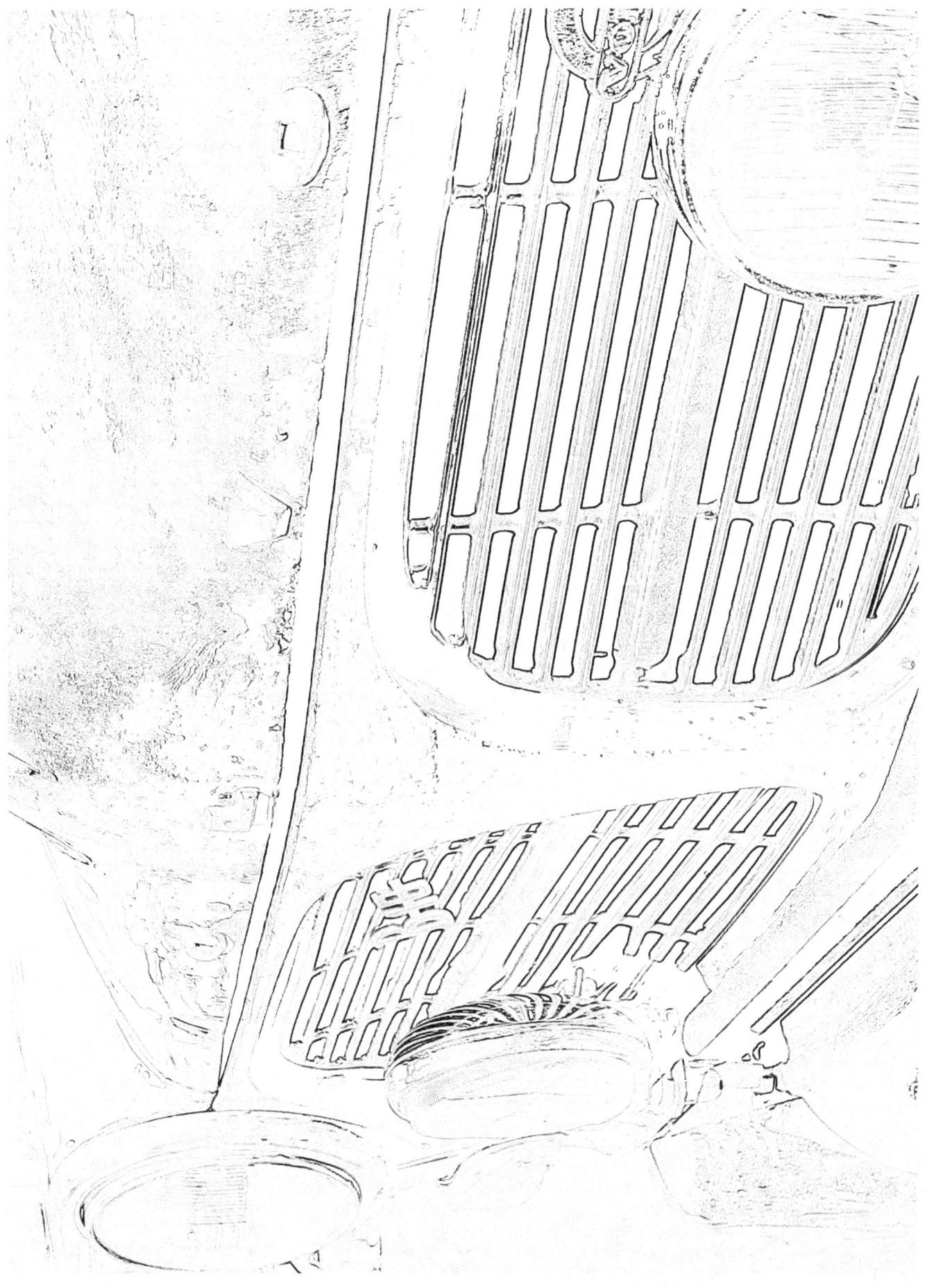

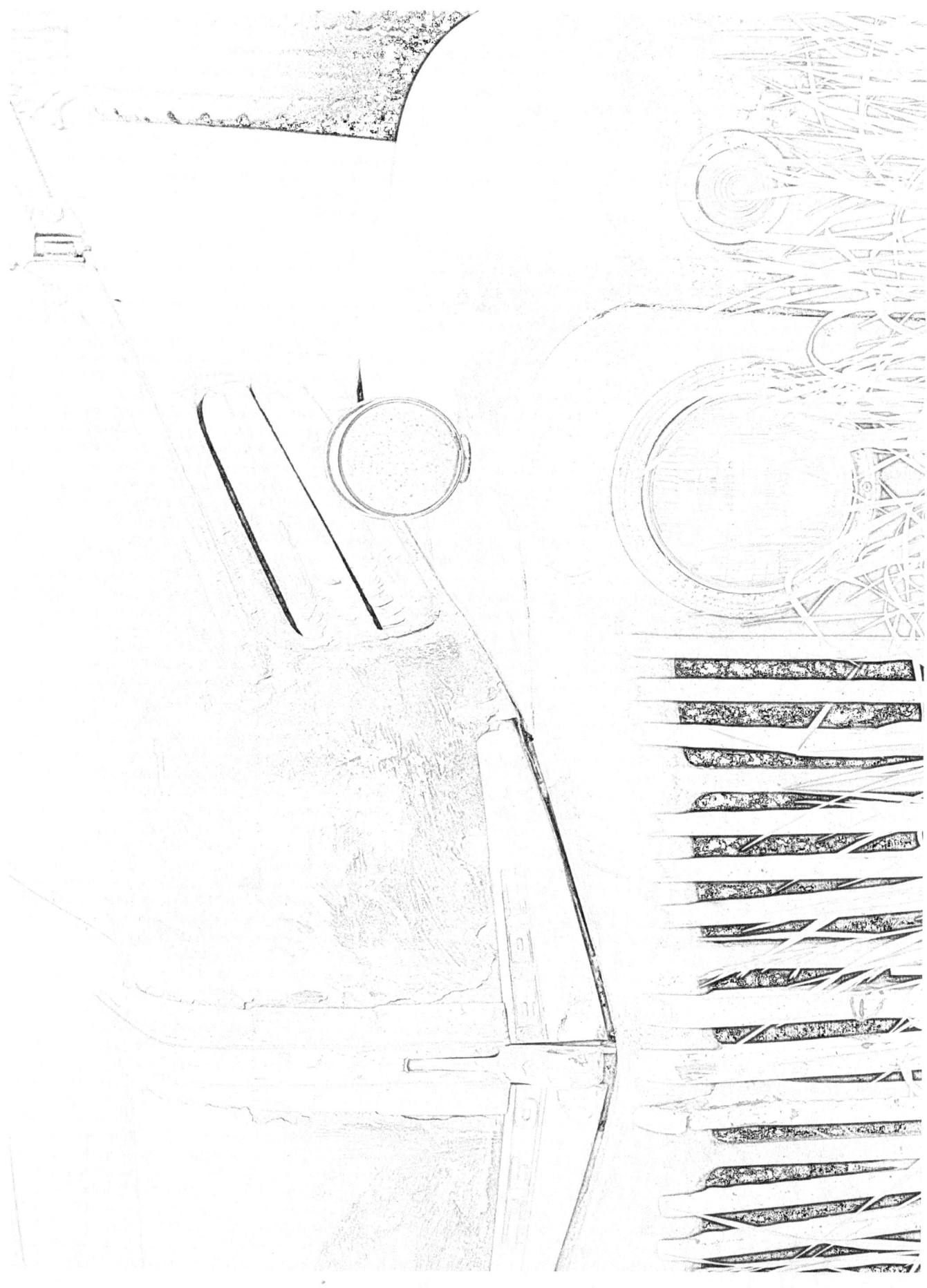

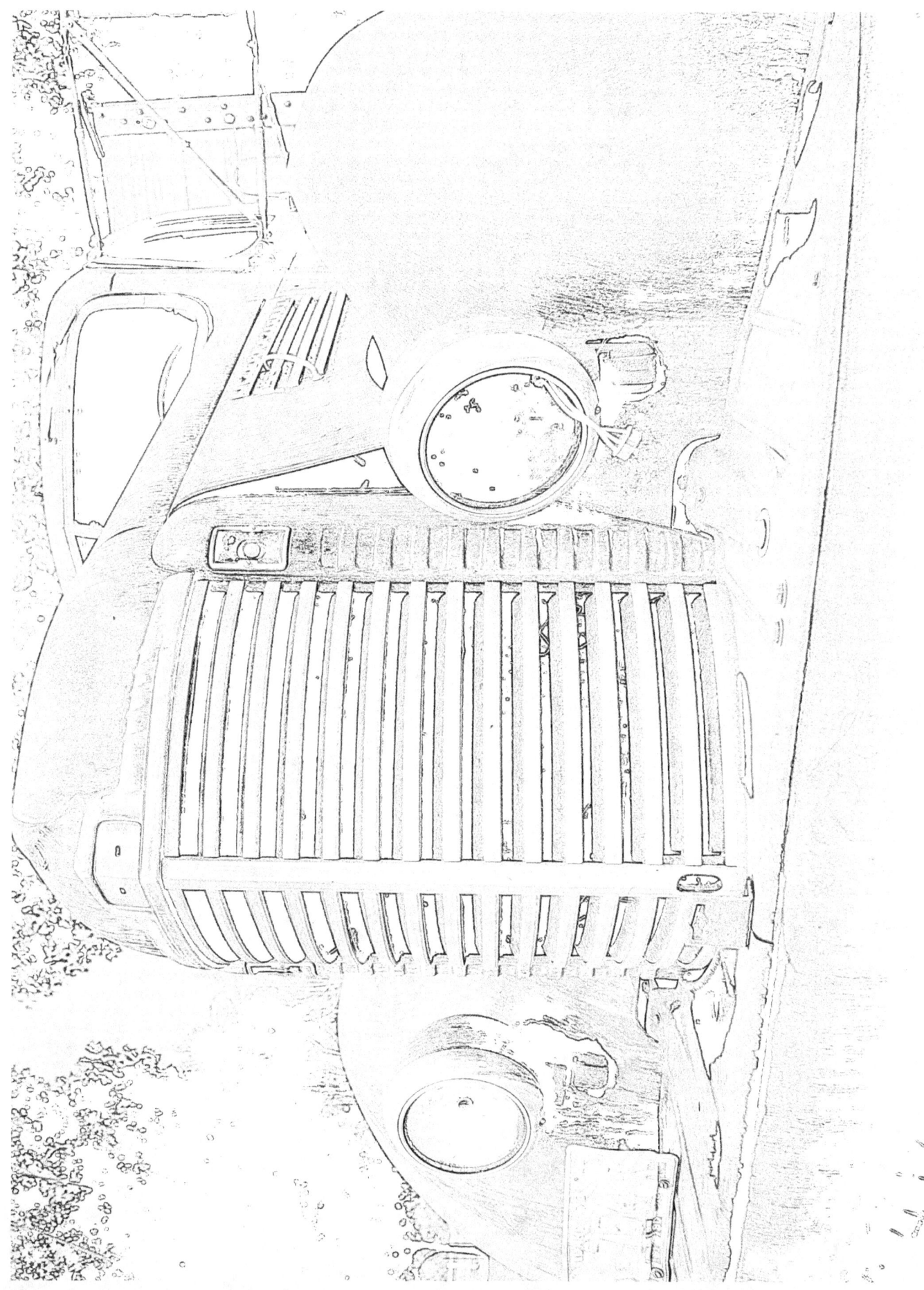

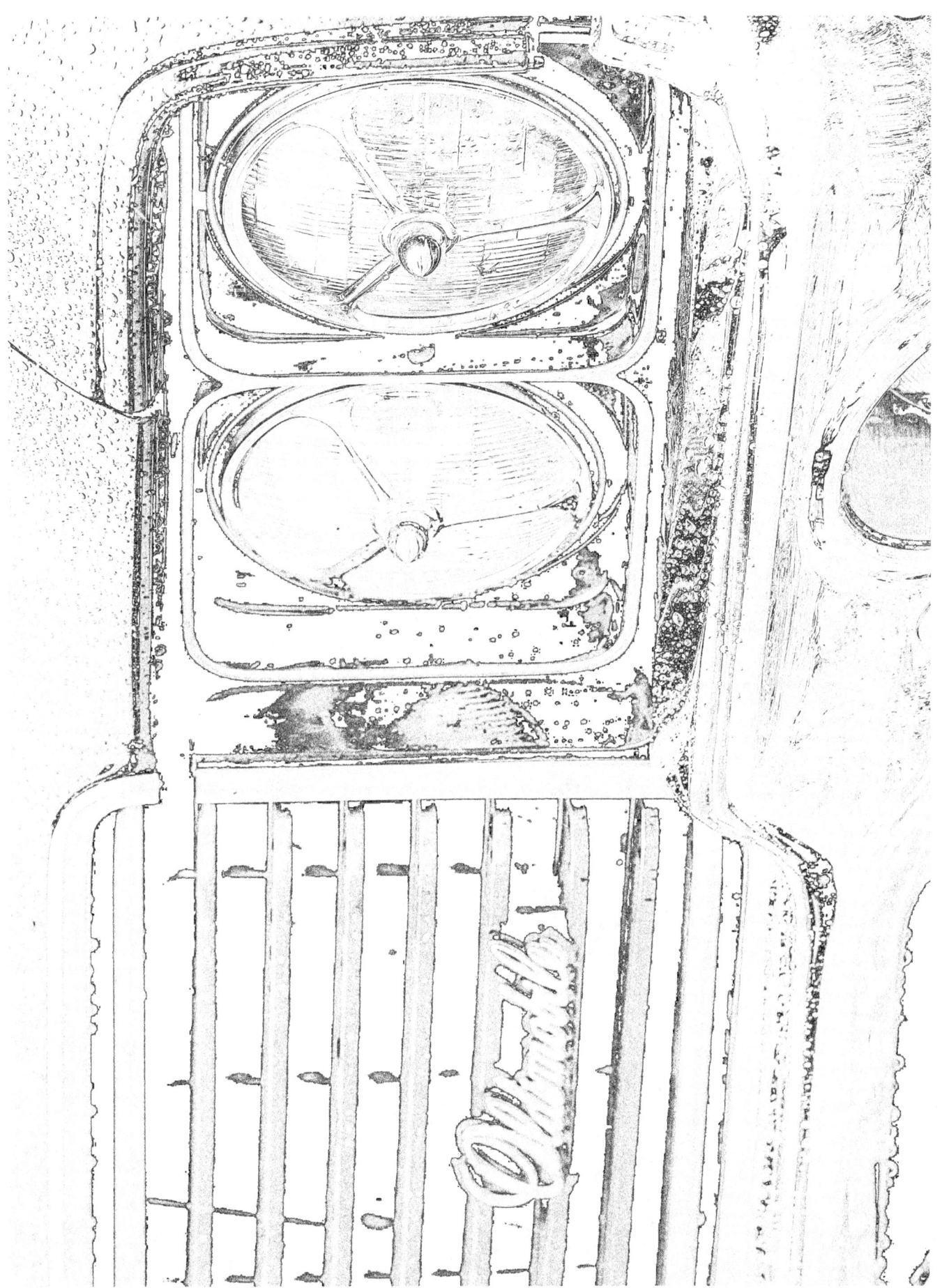

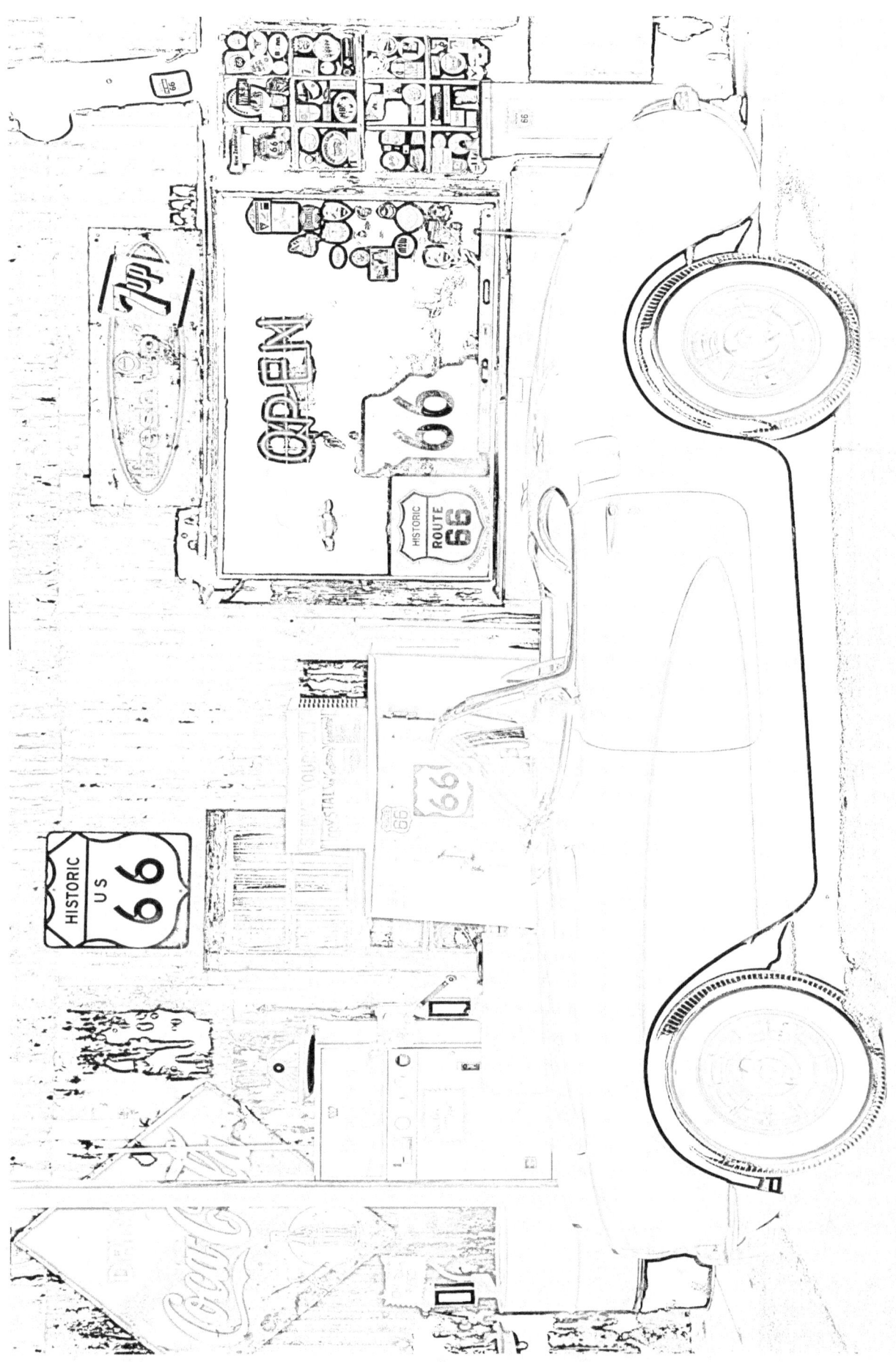

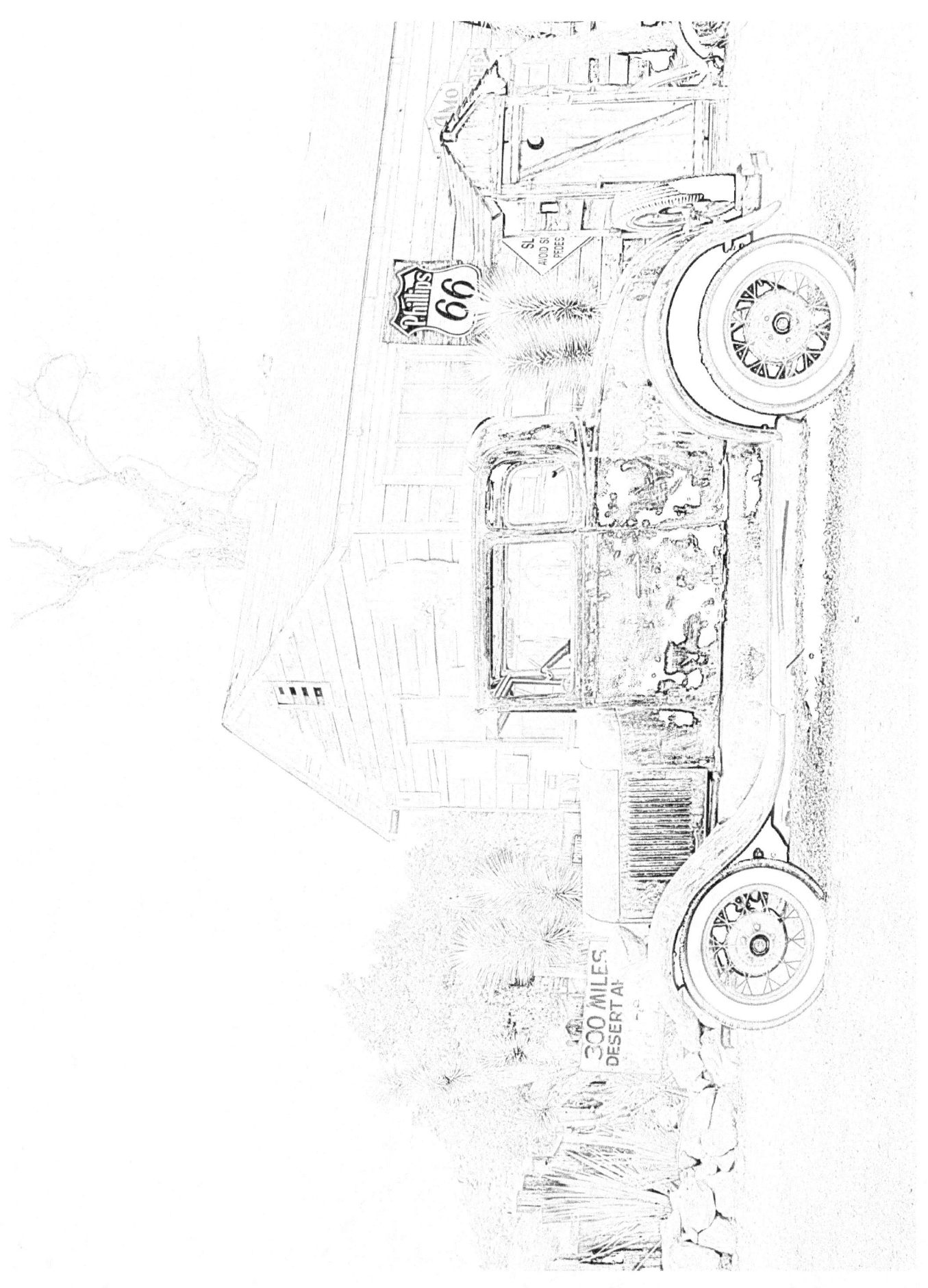

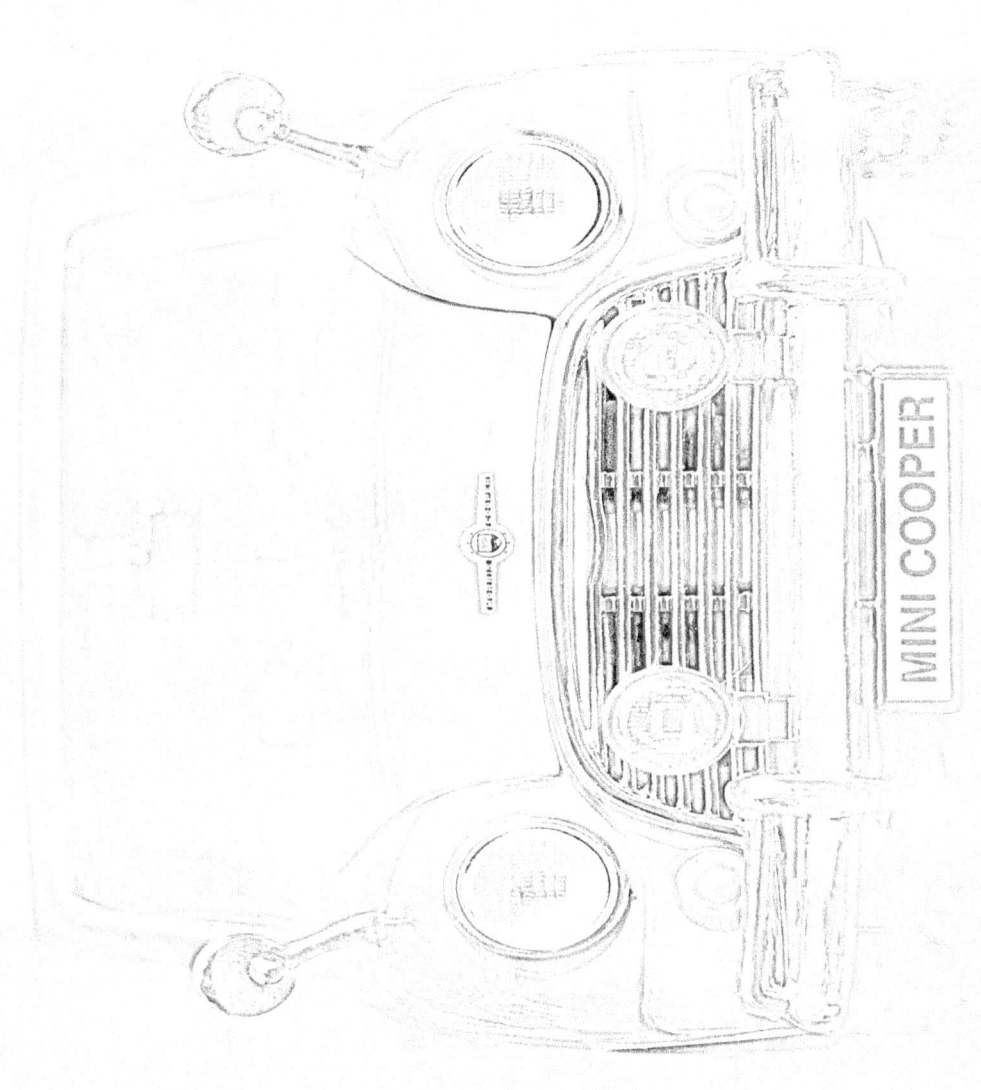

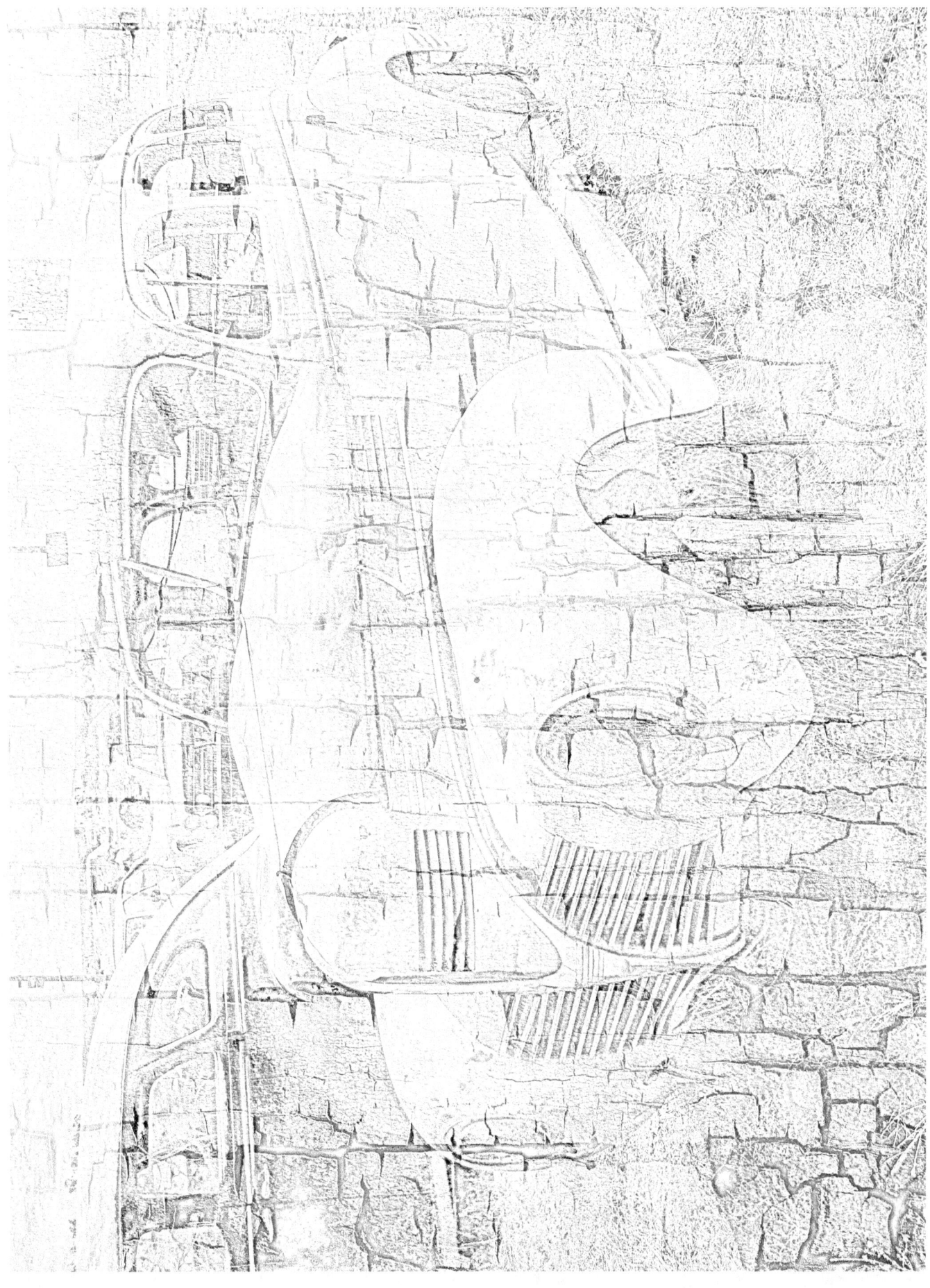

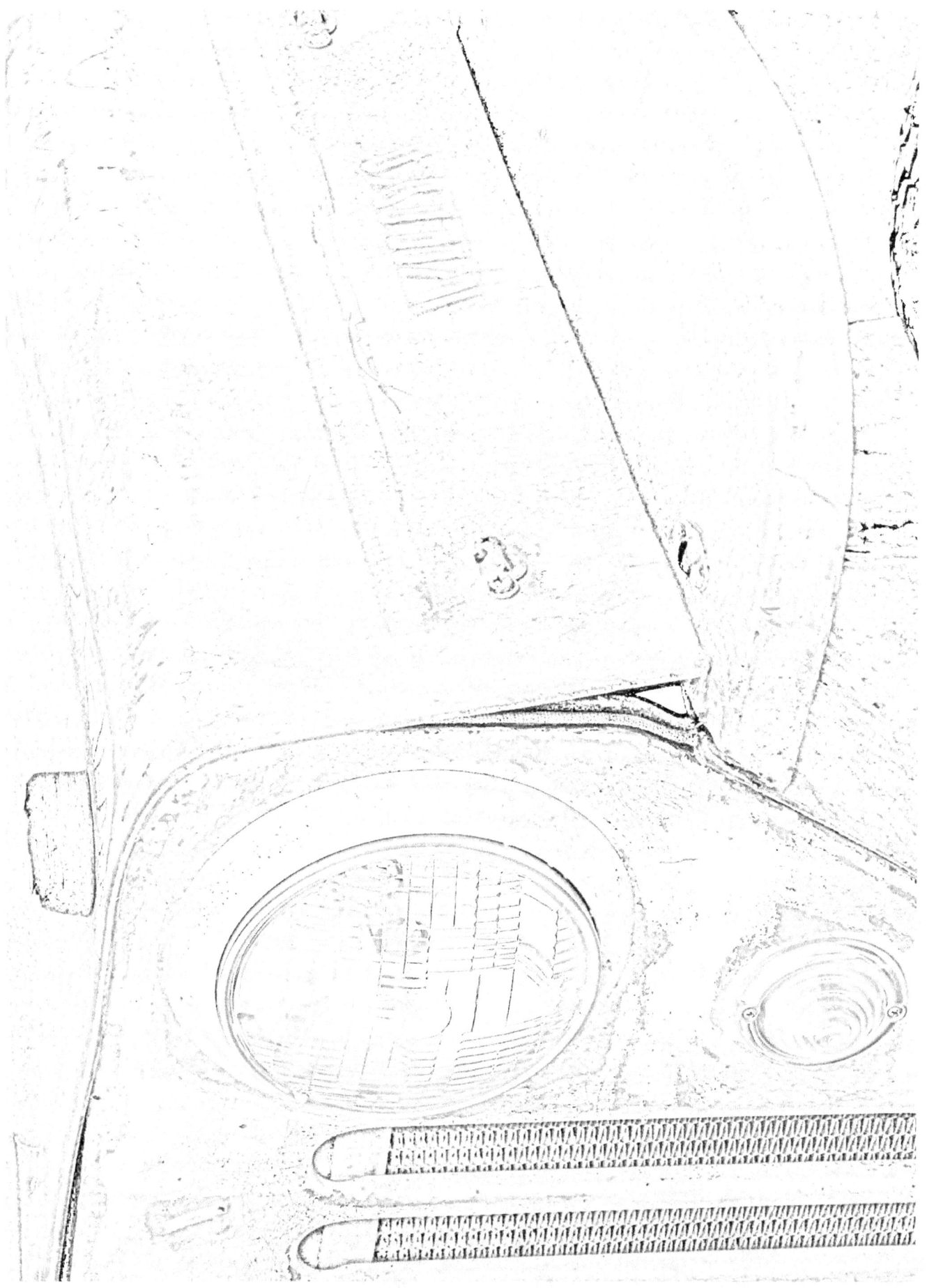

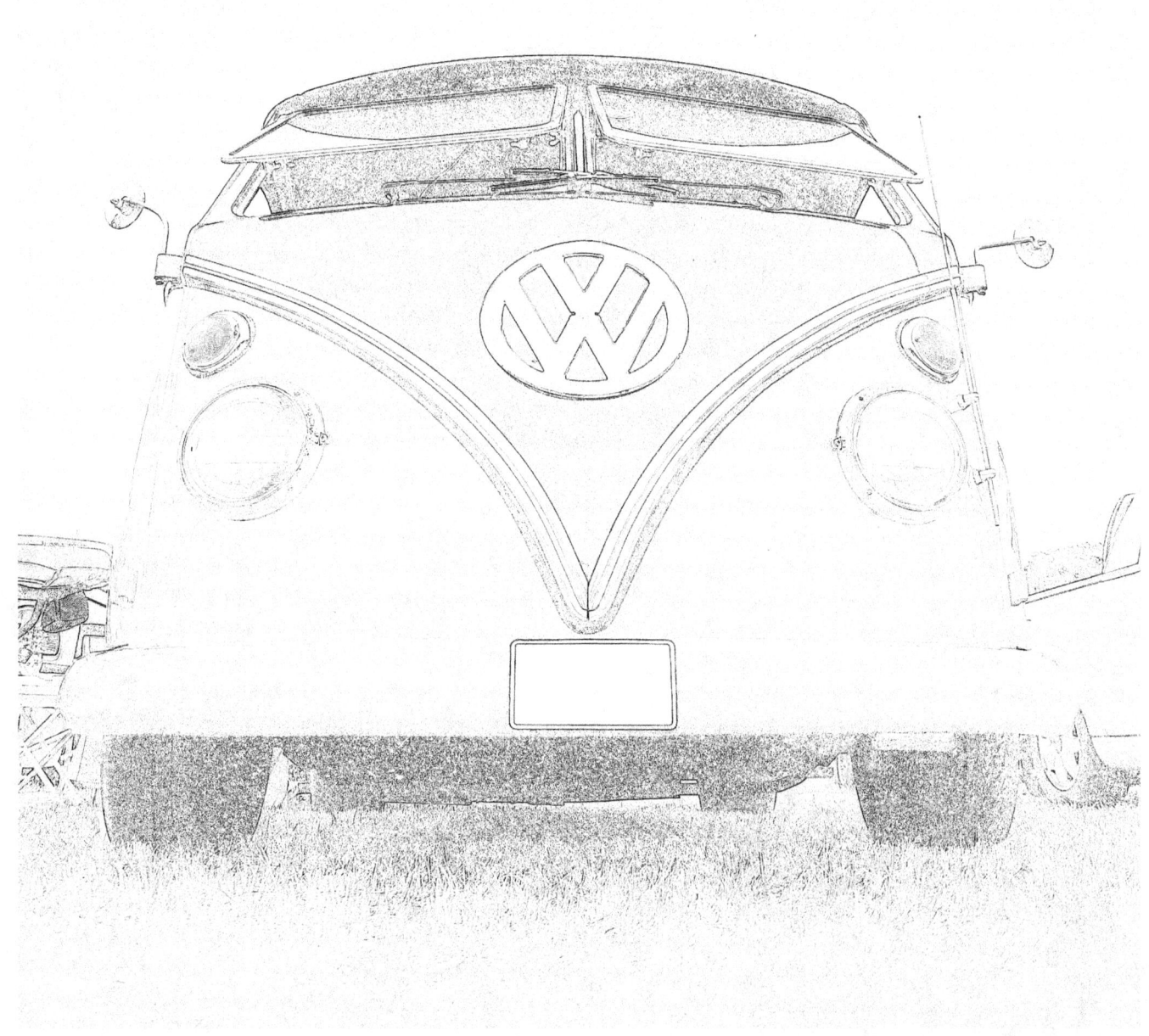

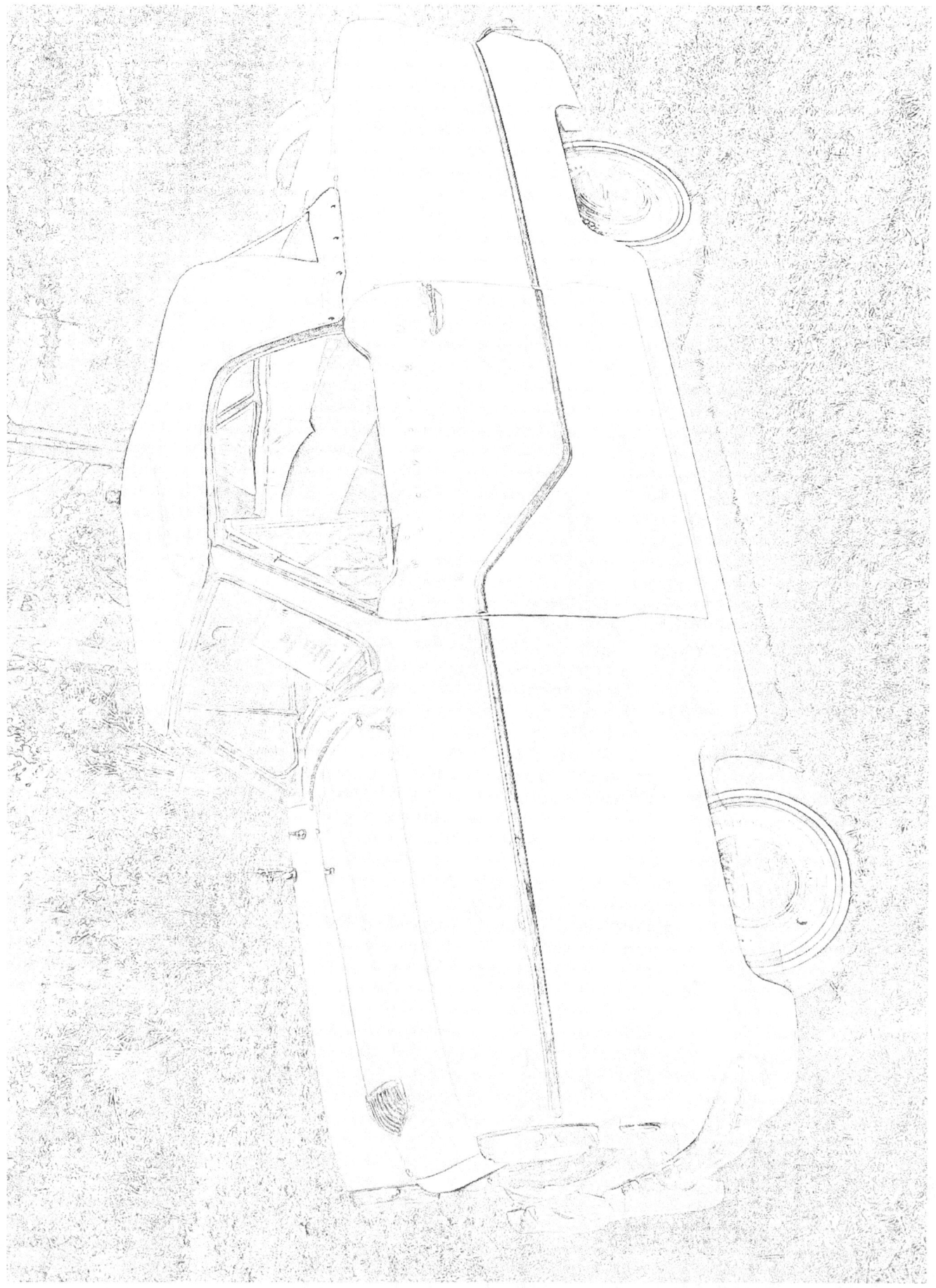

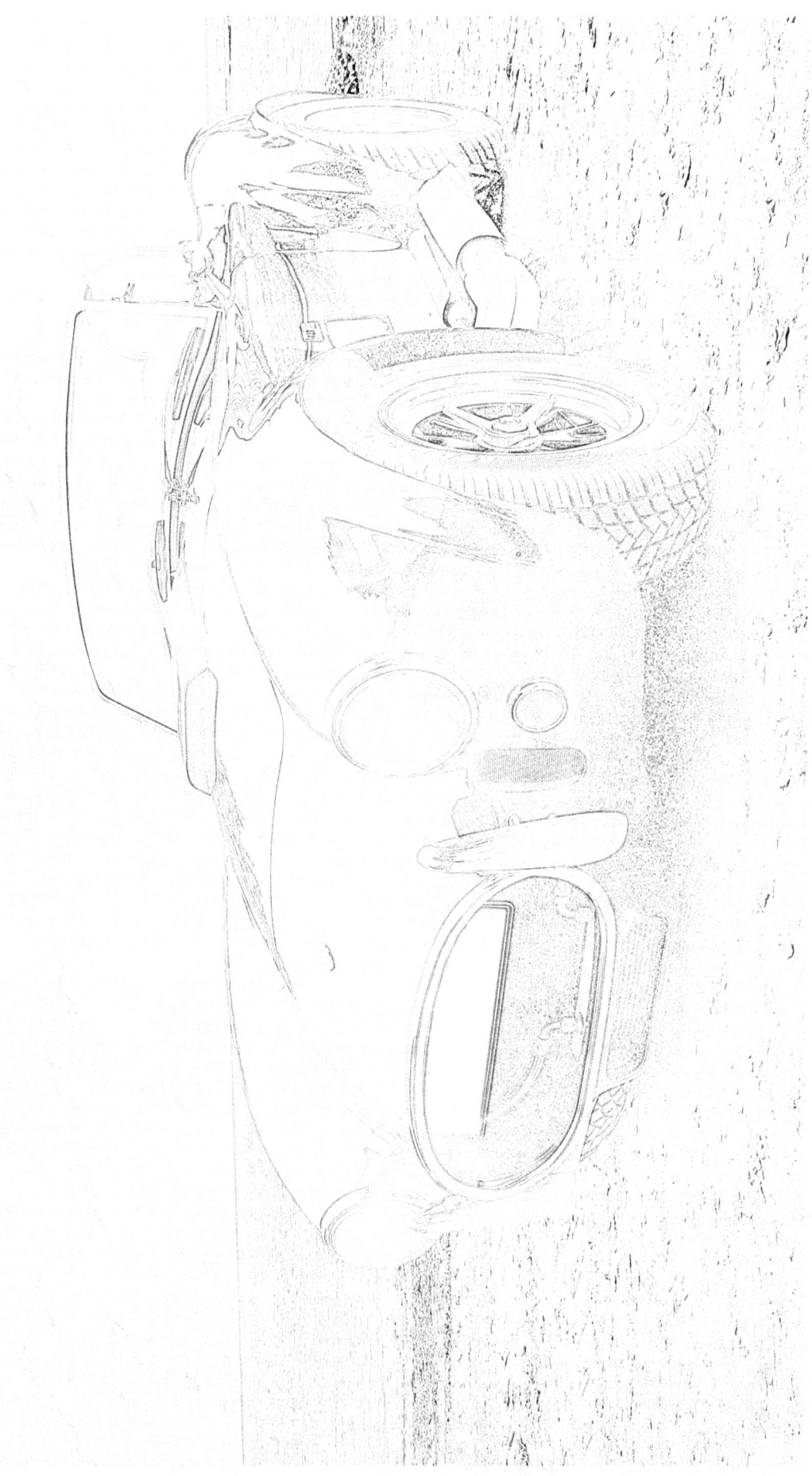

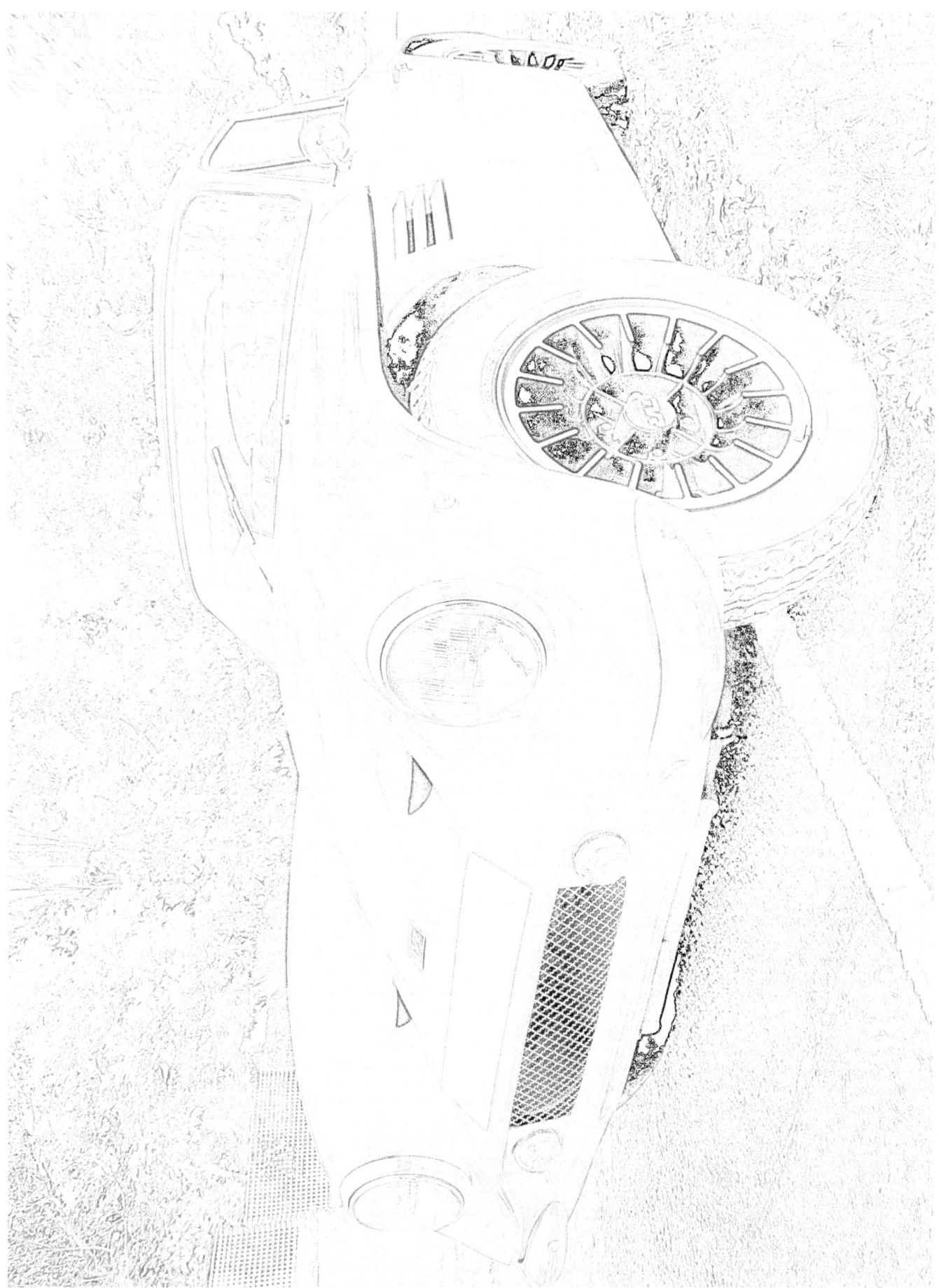

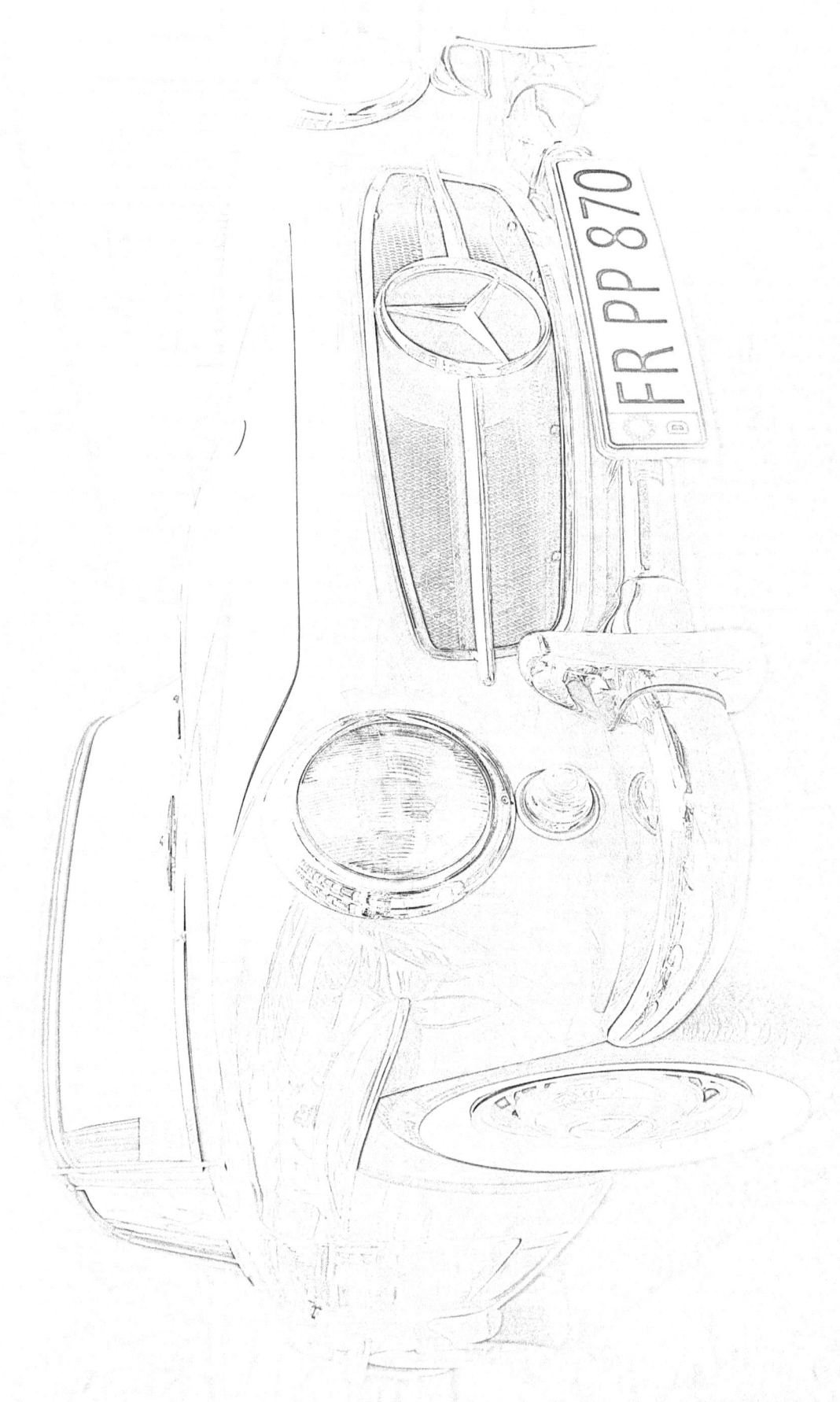

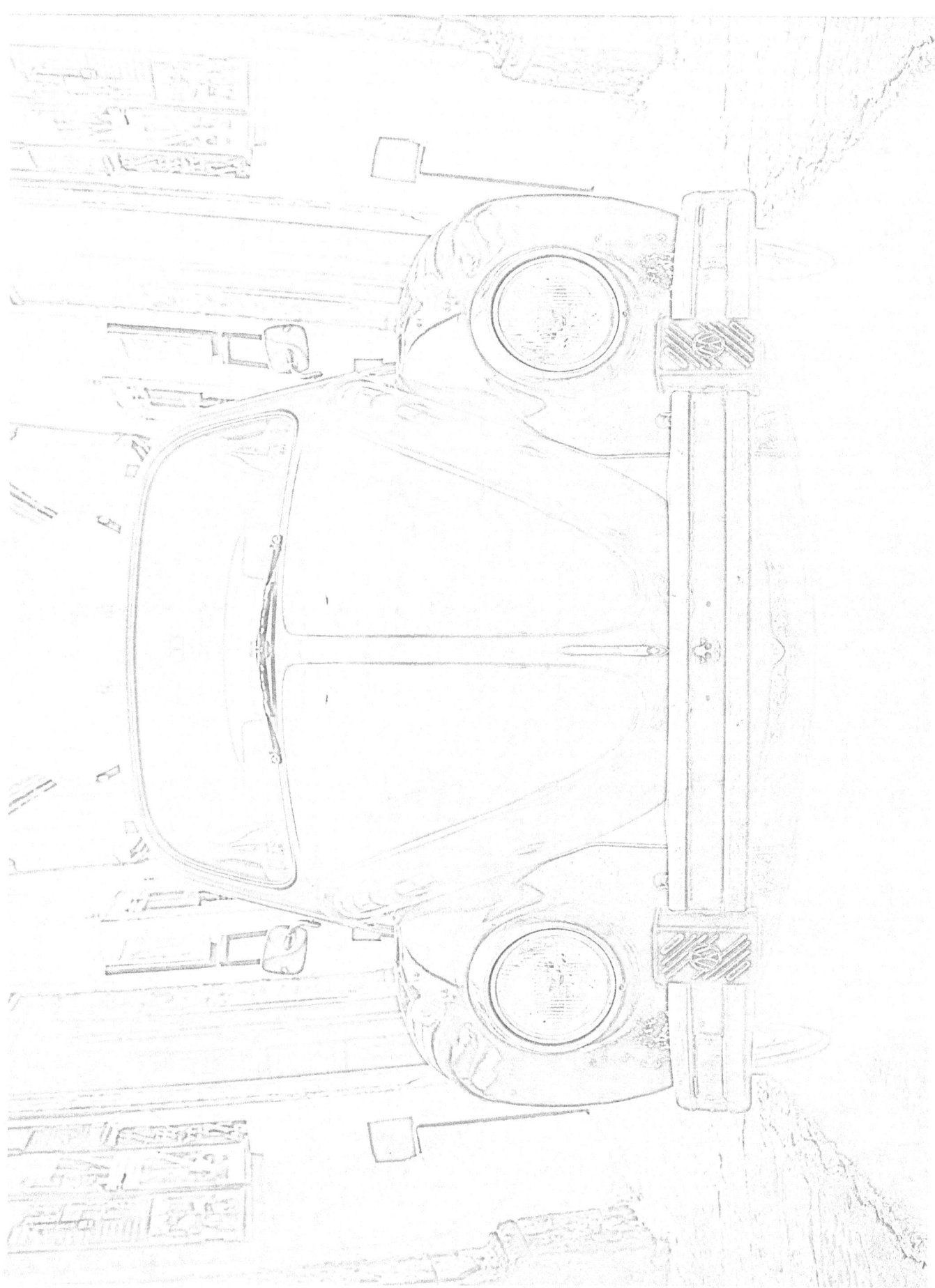

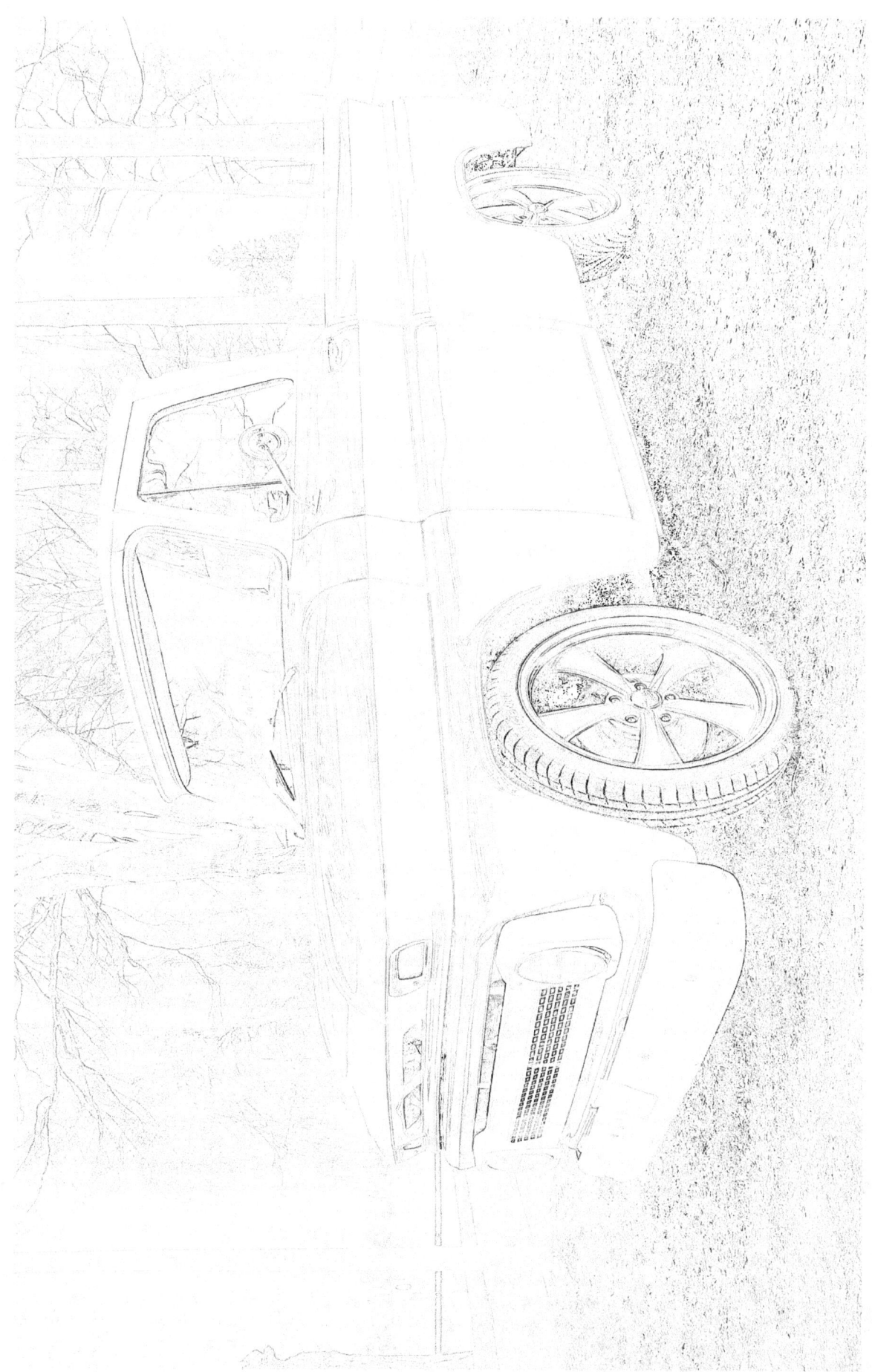

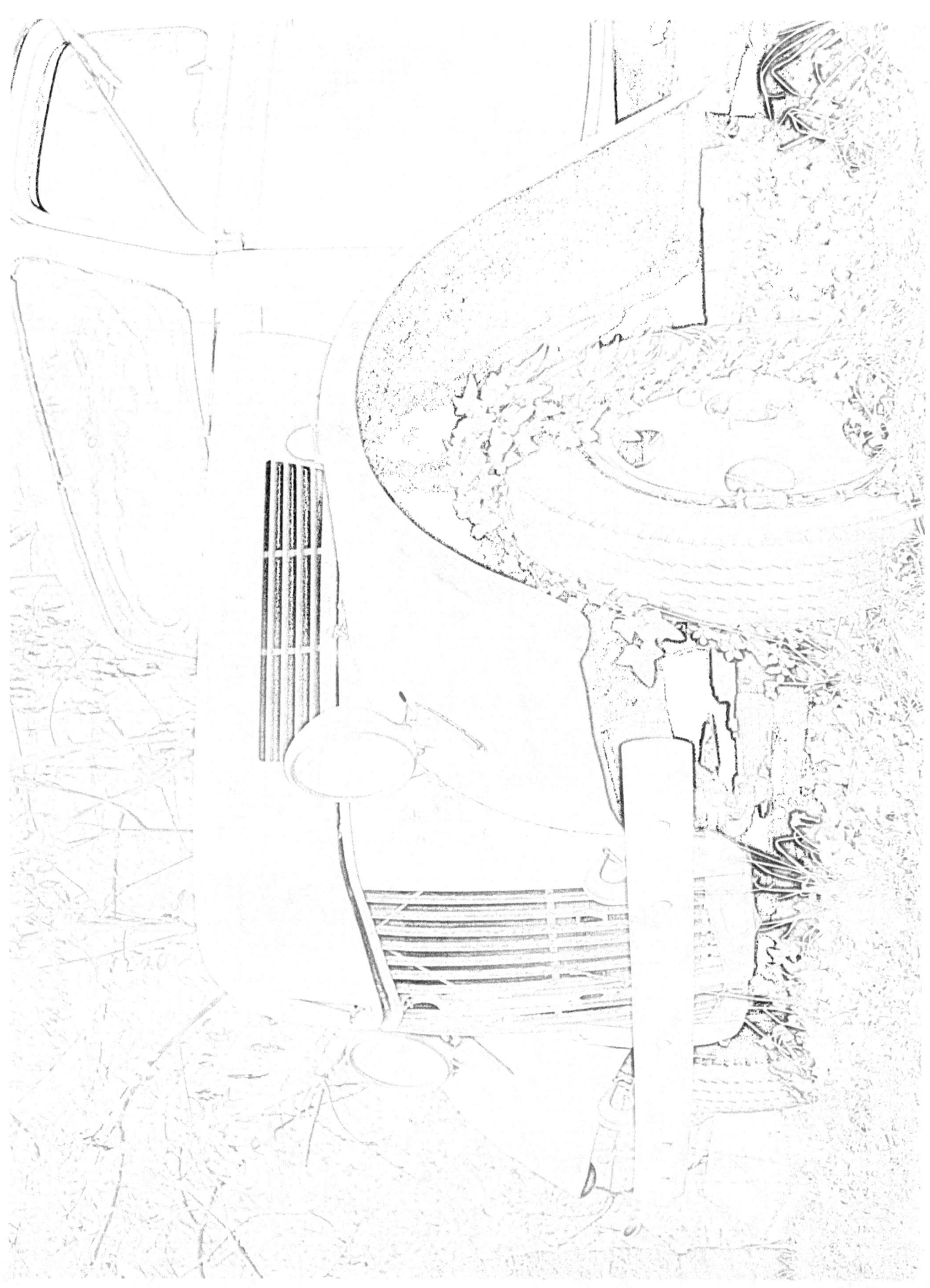

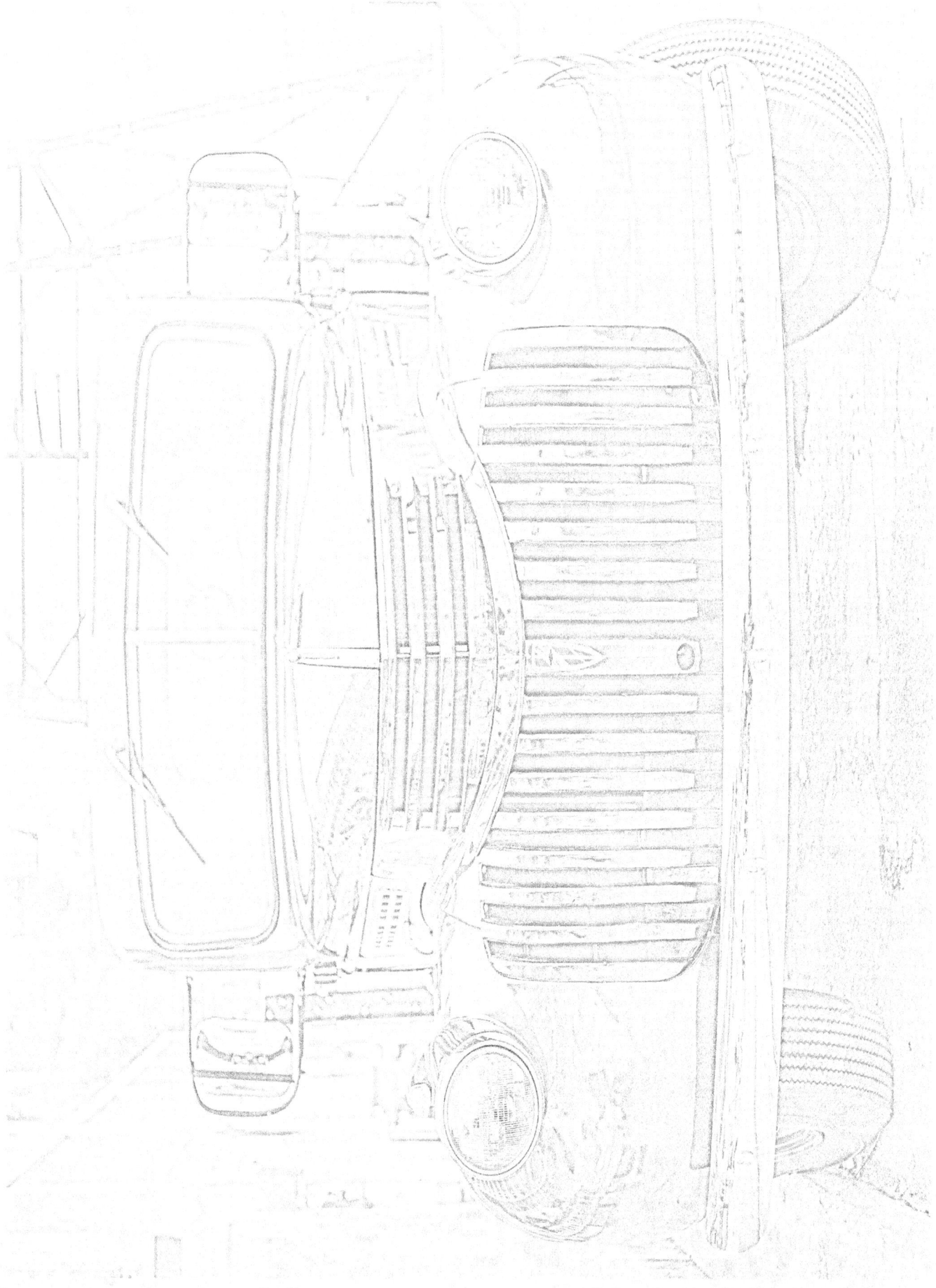

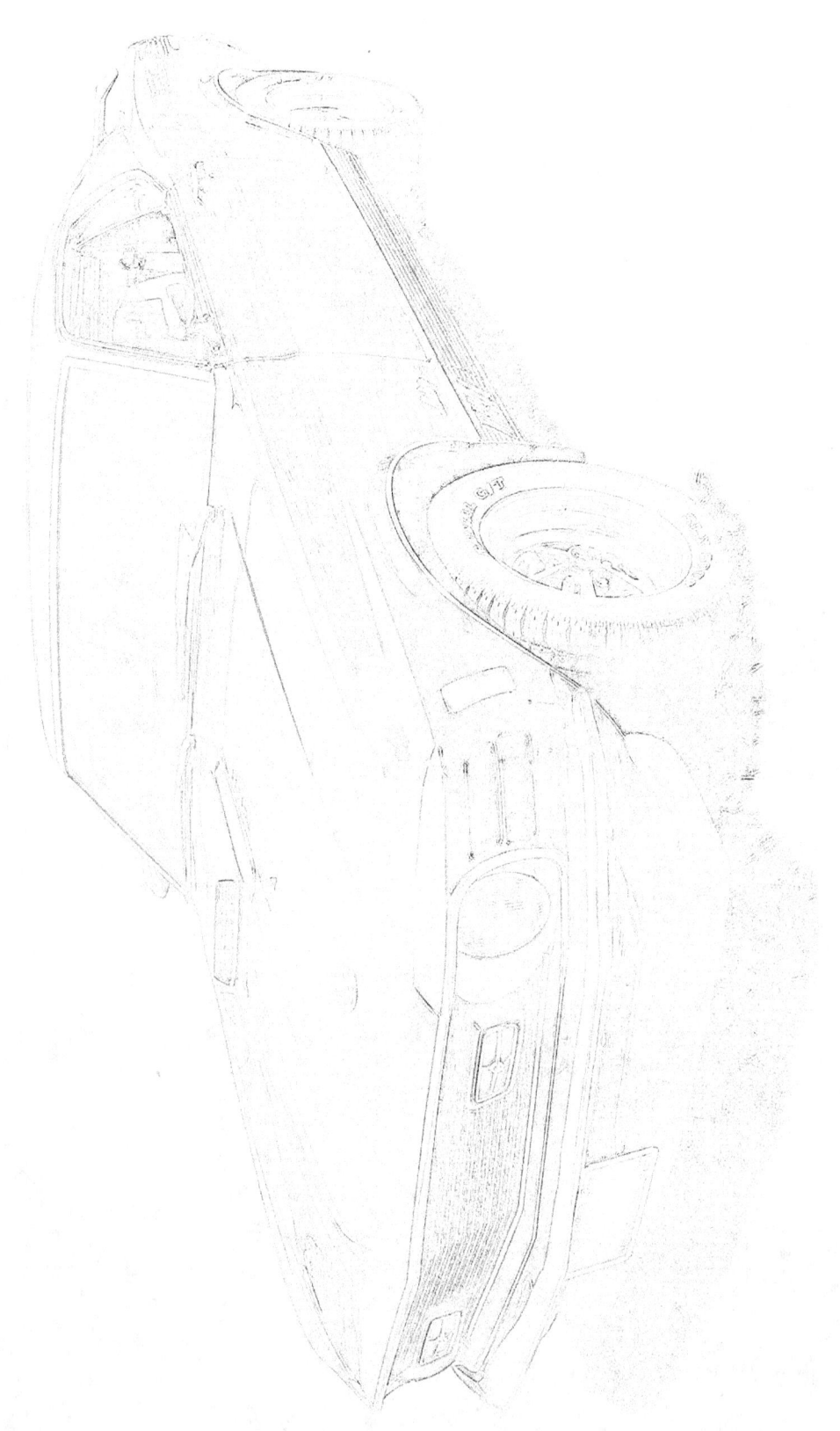

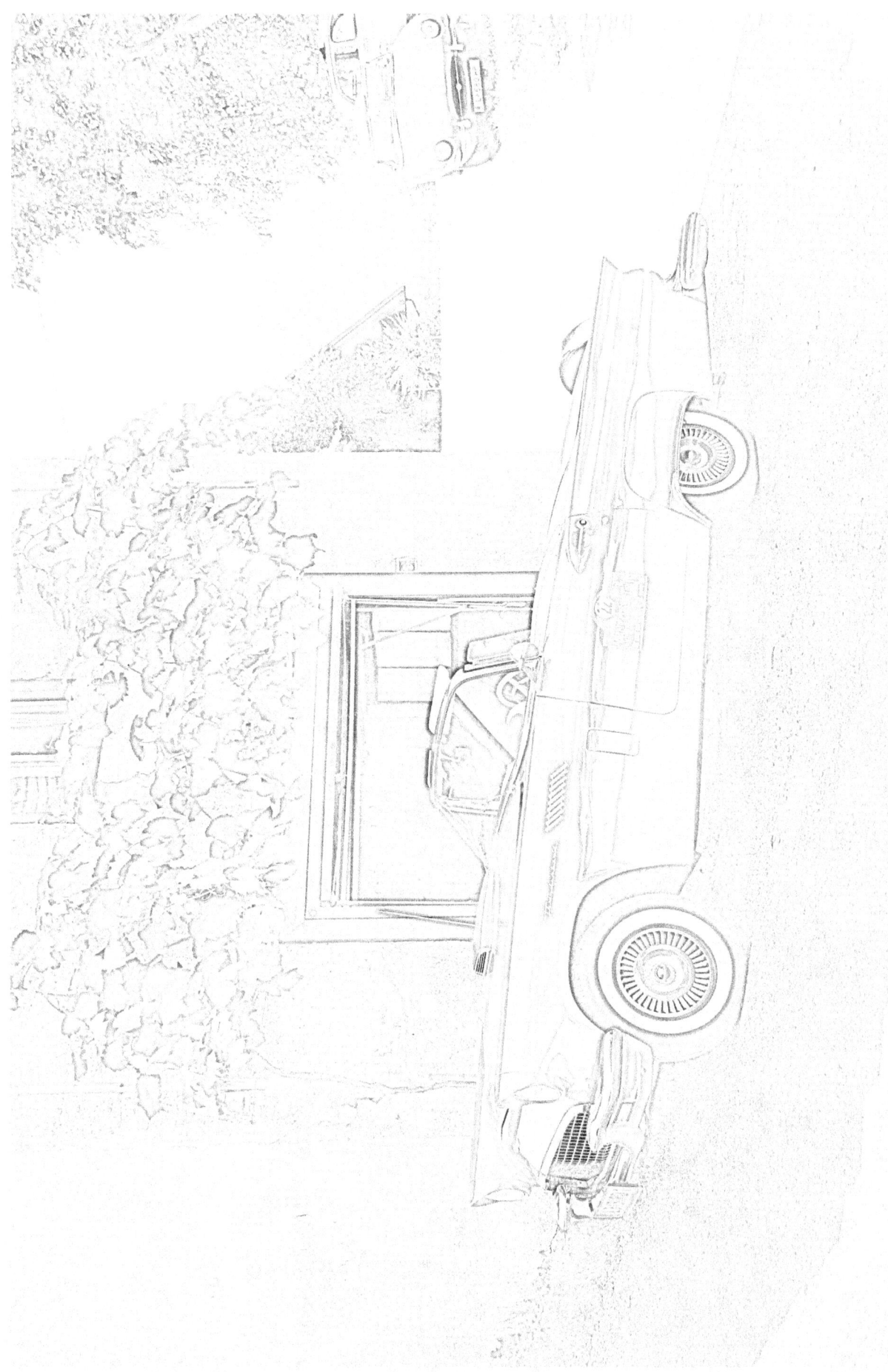

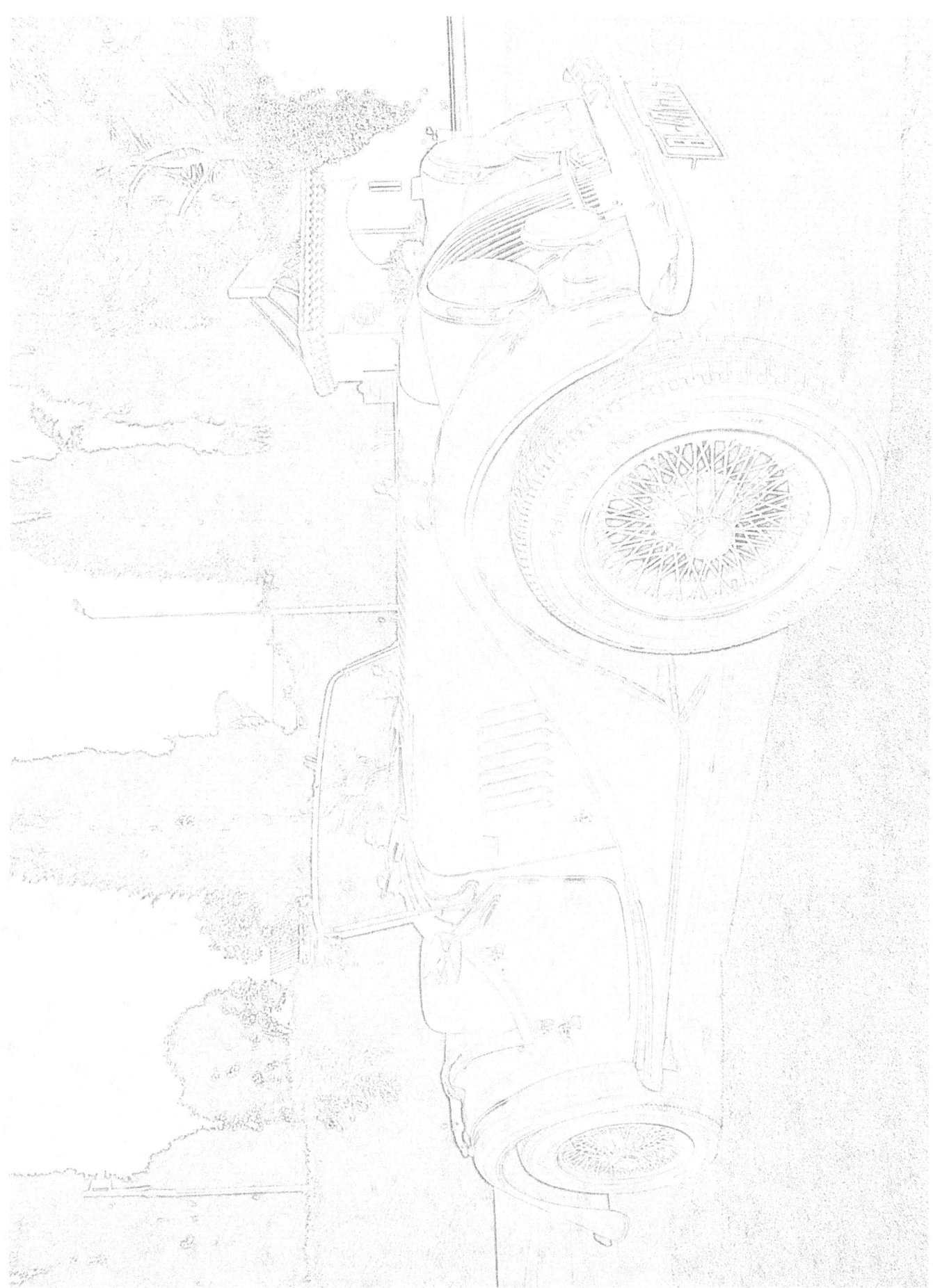

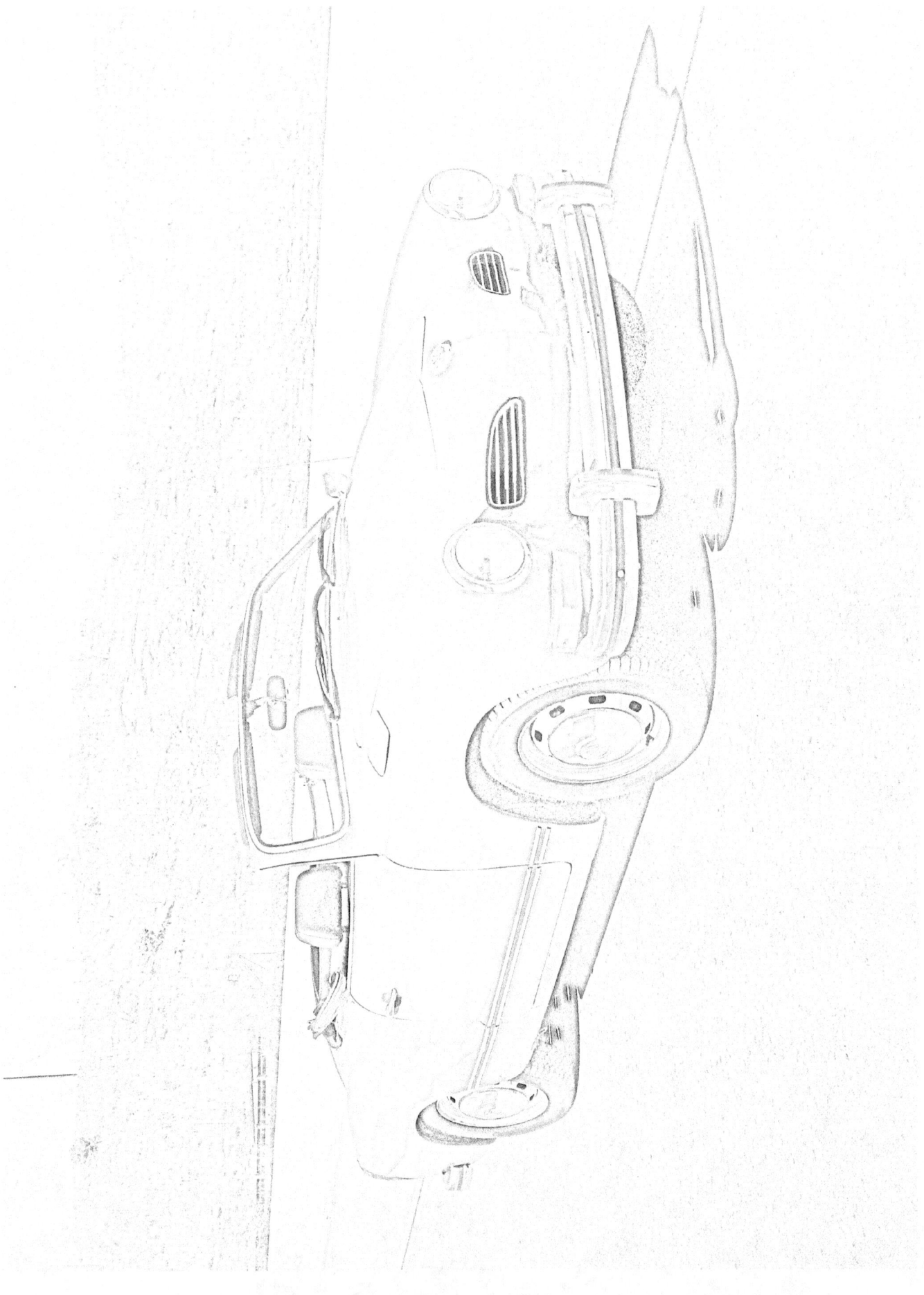

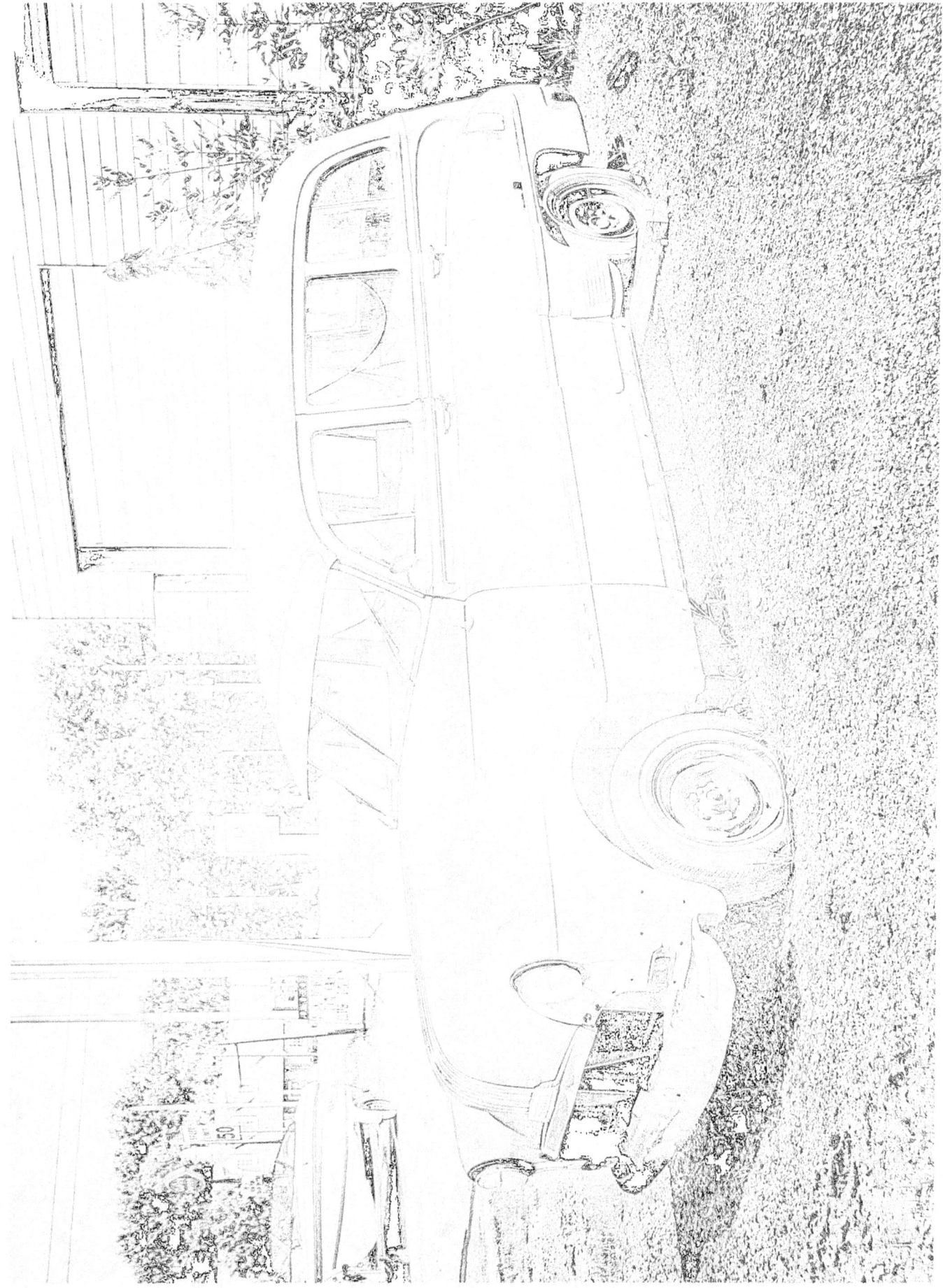

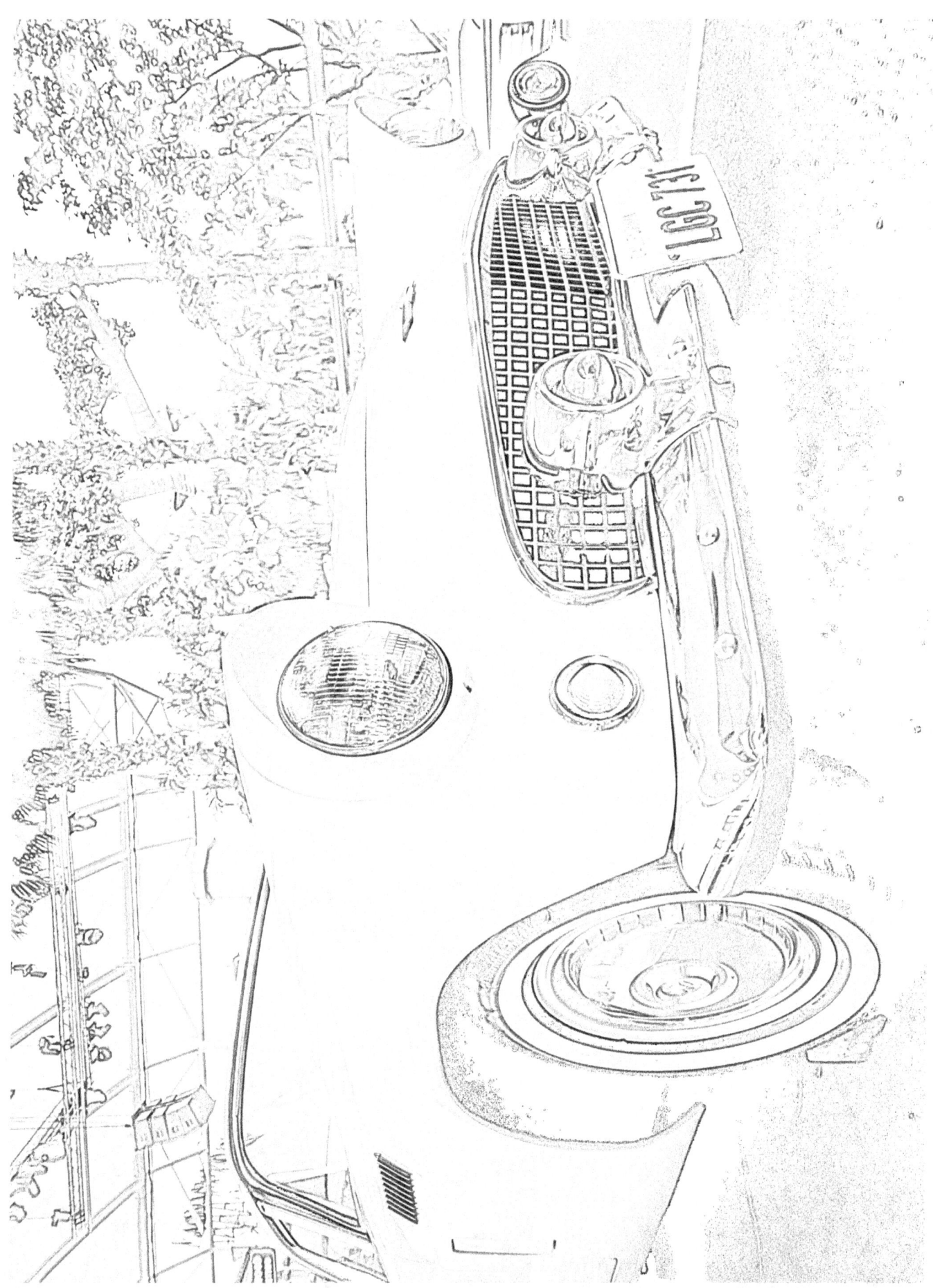

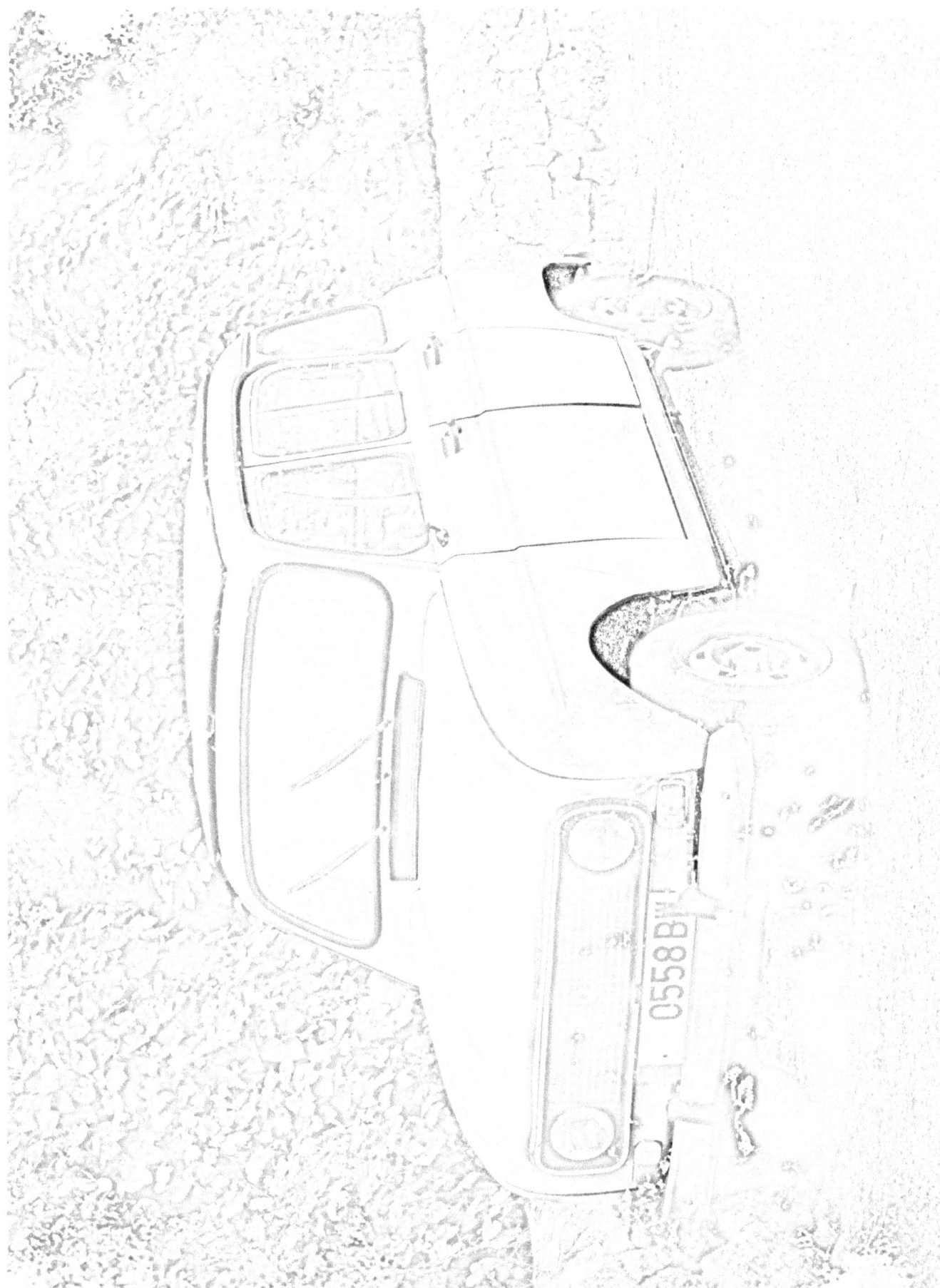

Thank you for ordering the *The Vintage Car And Truck Coloring Book Volume 1*! We hope you enjoyed it.

Volume 2 Is Coming Out Soon!

- Thanks again -

Don La Due

www.ingramcontent.com/pod-product-compliance
Lightning Source LLC
Chambersburg PA
CBHW081256180526
45170CB00007B/2450